KEYS
ON HOW TO BECOME
A BRAND

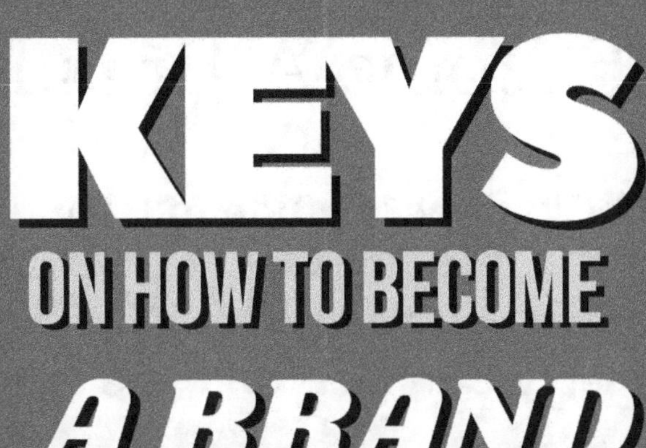

***10* BEGINNERS GUIDE TO BUILDING A SUCCESS STRATEGY THAT RESONATES AND DEEPLY CONNECTS WITH THE TARGET AUDIENCE"**

WRITTEN BY

DIANE A. GANDARA

Keys On How To Become A Brand:

"10 Beginners guide to Building a Success strategy that Resonates and deeply Connects with the target audience"

By

Diane A. Gandara

Copyright

Disclaimer

The information and advice handed in this book," Keys on How to Come a Brand," are grounded on the author's particular gestures and compliances. The author isn't a professional career counsel, and any conduct taken grounded on the content of this book are at the anthology's discretion. The author and publisher disclaim any liability for any direct, circular, or consequential loss or damage incurred by any anthology as a result of the use of any information or advice handed in this book.

While every trouble has been made to give accurate and over- to- date information, the fleetly changing nature of diligence and requests means that no guarantee can be given regarding the delicacy, punctuality, or connection of any of the contents. compendiums are encouraged to seek professional advice pertaining to their specific situations.

The citation of specific individualities, companies, products, or services in this book doesn't indicate countersign or recommendation by the author or publisher unless explicitly stated.

Table of Contents

<u>Introduction</u>:

Have you ever felt a desire for something greater, beyond the usual routine, but unsure where to start or hesitant to take the first step? Or have you ever wished you had a unique ability that makes you stand out like most people you have always admired? If that sounds like you, then you are at the right place.

Why you need this book

Imagine a scenario where you could make a form of yourself that everybody takes note of. Imagine having authority, or say a superpower that makes people notice you. Now, Consider the possibility that acting naturally could be your own unique move. Oh yeah! This book isn't just about having an effect; rather, it's about being somebody individuals generally adore. Prepared to make your own principles for progress?

Indeed, "Keys On how to become a brand" is the right manual for that! Your guide to a day to day existence where you can have a major effect and everybody knows it, More like having a wise friend guide you through the process of creating a brand that truly resonates with people.

Your brand becomes an authentic expression of who you are, more than just a logo or catchy phrase.

In providing a glimpse into the book, I want to convey that there's a valuable brand within you waiting to be recognized. I don't want to detail the content's richness of this book, as it's more rewarding for you to explore and experience the results by following the keys revealed in different pages. Please, I repeat, ensure you diligently utilize the keys unveiled in this book as it combines insights from various paid resources, including classes and courses that cost at least $500 thereby making every page of this book to be very important, therefore, as you flip through the pages, you'll realize that it's not only about your story but also about understanding others. Now, the question is, What do people genuinely care about? What messages resonate with them? Your brand becomes part of their story, woven into their everyday struggles and victories. share your journey, wins, and even setbacks.

As you digest this book, you will understand why criticisms are not obstacles; rather you should view them as signs pointing you in the right direction. you will also understand that Networking isn't just about exchanging business cards; it's about connecting with people who understand and enhance your brand. Attending events, joining groups will make your brand part of a larger conversation.

You will again understand why continuous improvement is essential in a rapidly evolving world. And that would Propel you to Stay informed, learn, and share your knowledge. Success isn't the end; it grows with feedback. So Seek reviews, appreciate your audience and make them part of your brand's evolution.

Here's what to expect after reading this book to the end

- ***You will learn how to uncover Your Distinct Identity:*** Explore the strategies that distinguish successful individuals, empowering you to carve out a unique identity in a world teeming with competition.

- ***You will learn how to Boost Your Confidence***: Acquire insights and tools to conquer self-doubt, granting you the confidence to shine and stand out in various facets of your life.

- ***You will learn how to navigate the Competitive world:*** Discover practical, game-changing strategies to traverse the saturated world, leaving an enduring and impactful impression.

- ***You will learn how to Propel Beyond the Ordinary:*** Transform the ordinary into the extraordinary by implementing strategies that propel you beyond the commonplace, establishing yourself as a force to be reckoned with.

- ***You will Gain mastery for Personal Branding***: Embark on a transformative journey to master the art of personal branding, ensuring you make a mark that resonates both personally and professionally.

- *You will learn how to Amplify Your Influence:* Decipher the intricacies of influence, gaining tools that I have listed out as Recommended Resources at the last page of this book,these tools are not only to capture attention but also to create a ripple effect in your social and professional circles.

- *You will Stand Out from the Crowd*: Learn the art of standing out in a world filled with noise, thereby making a magnetic impact to ensure your message and presence are both noticed and remembered.

- *You will learn Practical Strategies for Success:* Acquire a practical and actionable treasure map of strategies guiding you toward unparalleled success in your journey for growth.

- ***And Finally you will Become Your Destined Brand:***

As you know, this book serves as a guiding companion to help you become the brand you were destined to be, underscoring the pivotal role your personal brand plays in achieving extraordinary success.

"Keys on how to Become a Brand" isn't just a consumption of information; it's a challenge and a call to action to unlock the doors to your unique identity, and also an empowering journey that equips you with tools and insights to stand out, succeed, and craft a lasting legacy.

The keys are in your hands; let the journey begin!

Bonus!

Practical ways to Utilize AI ChatGPT Prompts for generating the Right Responses and a Step by Step Guide for Business/Brand Profile Creations

See Page 25-28

And Page 63-68

Key Number one

Self-Reflection

•Recognize your assets, abilities, and values,

Embarking on the initial chapter of the meditative journey, let's take a moment to delve into the core concept of "Keys to Becoming a Brand." This is an invitation to unravel the essence of transforming oneself into a brand, a journey transcending mere existence and altering self-perception. Interested? Let's commence with self-reflection.

The bedrock of any impactful brand lies in self-discovery and self-awareness. Consider this gentle reminder: each individual possesses a unique identity that distinguishes them from the crowd. Self-reflection is akin to a personal adventure, a contemplative exploration to unearth one's strengths and competencies. It's akin to a cozy introspective conversation, a mirror for one's thoughts and emotions.

NOW! TAKE A DEEP BREATH

Begin by identifying your strengths – those standout qualities that set you apart. Whether you excel at problem-solving, possess exceptional communication skills, or bring humor to others, these are your strengths. Proceed to contemplate your learned skills, whether it's coding proficiency, culinary expertise, or organizational finesse. Don't overlook your values, the principles that hold significance for you. Whether honesty or kindness resonates deeply, these are your values and the core beliefs shaping your identity. Take a moment, savor a cup of coffee, and explore the unique qualities that make you shine!

Strengths represent your exceptional abilities making people laugh or adept problem-solving. Skills encompass the practical talents you've acquired, whether in gaming, cooking, or academic assistance. Values are akin to personal principles, reflecting what truly matters to you. Whether it's honesty, kindness, or a penchant for exploration, these are your values, the foundational elements of self-awareness. Let's delve further into this essence of self-awareness.

There Are Two Types of Self-Awareness

Over the past five decades, researchers have applied diverse definitions to the concept of self-awareness. Some view it as the capacity to monitor our internal thoughts, while others characterize it as a transient state of self-consciousness. Another perspective defines it as the dissonance between our self-perception and how others perceive us.

To move forward in understanding how to enhance self-awareness, it became essential to consolidate these findings and establish a comprehensive definition. Across our examinations of various studies, two primary facets of self-awareness consistently surfaced.

The first, termed internal self-awareness, reflects the clarity with which we perceive our own values, passions, aspirations, alignment with our environment, reactions (including thoughts, feelings, behaviors, strengths, and weaknesses), and impact on others. Research indicates that internal self-awareness correlates with elevated job and relationship satisfaction, personal and social control, and happiness. Conversely, it exhibits a negative correlation with anxiety, stress, and depression.

The second facet, external self-awareness, involves understanding how others perceive us across the same dimensions mentioned earlier. Our findings reveal that individuals aware of how others perceive them demonstrate enhanced empathy and an ability to adopt others' perspectives. Leaders who comprehend how their employees view them tend to foster better relationships, increased satisfaction, and a general perception of effectiveness.

It might be assumed that high internal self-awareness corresponds with high external self-awareness. However, our research found virtually no relationship between them. Consequently, we identify four leadership archetypes, each offering distinct opportunities for improvement:

•*Seekers*: Low internal and external self-awareness. They are yet to understand themselves, their values, or how their teams perceive them, potentially leading to feelings of stagnation or frustration.

•*Pleasers*: Low internal self-awareness but high external self-awareness. Their focus on how they appear to others might cause them to overlook their own priorities, resulting in choices not aligned with personal success and fulfillment.

•***Introspective***: High internal self-awareness but low external self-awareness. While clear about their identity, they may neglect to challenge their views or seek feedback from others, which can negatively impact relationships and limit success.

•***Aware Individuals***: High internal and external self-awareness. They possess a clear understanding of themselves, their goals, and actively seek and value others' opinions. This is where leaders fully realize the profound benefits of self-awareness.

In simpler terms, self-reflection boils down to taking a moment to ponder your strengths, capabilities, values, and public perception. It's akin to getting acquainted with the fantastic person you are. Now, let's put this into practice. Gather your writing materials and jot down all the unique aspects of your identity, encompassing your innate abilities and acquired skills. Now, proceed to organize them based on their visibility, consider those actions that garner applause, the things you effortlessly excel at, perhaps even activities you may not deem significant.

•*Highlight what makes you special..*

Identify what you excel in, what comes naturally to you, and what makes you feel celebrated. If given the resources and an opportunity to engage in just one activity on Earth before your demise, what would that be? Take the time to contemplate these aspects.

By answering these questions, you are on the brink of evolving into the brand that your world has been anticipating.

Key Number Two

Characterize Your Image

What defines a brand is its distinctive blend of a name, symbol, or design, setting it apart in consumers' eyes. More than just a logo, it encapsulates a business's identity and perception. Brands aim to create lasting impressions tied to unique qualities and experiences.

In a traditional sense, branding is the deliberate process of shaping and maintaining a brand. It entails crafting a unified identity for a product, service, or company, covering aspects like name, logo, design, and messaging. The objective is to build a strong, positive connection in consumers' minds, fostering trust, recognition, and loyalty. This extends beyond tangible elements to emotional and perceptual bonds with the brand.Now, let's apply this concept to you:

Target Audience and Competitors:

Identify your target audience and competitors. Define your focus and personality to stand out.

Business/Brand Name: Choose a name that resonates with your identity and message.

Slogan: Craft a memorable slogan that encapsulates your essence and resonates with your audience.

Vision and Mission: Define your vision and mission. If needed, utilize AI assistance at chat.openai.com for generating compelling statements aligning with your brand. Keep in mind that the crucial aspect involves crafting a distinct and genuine representation that aligns with your strengths and messaging. For instance, when interacting with AI ChatGPT, you can prompt it by stating your brand name and the nature of your business.

(BONUS I)

Ask the AI to generate a mission statement for your brand, then submit or use the arrow sign to send the request. If the response doesn't meet your expectations, you have the option to regenerate. For convenient access on mobile devices, consider downloading the app. Refer to appendix 1 for the AI ChatGPT interface, where you can sign up and utilize prompts to generate your content freely. To get started, open your web browser and visit "chat.openai.com."

See Appendix 1 in the bonus page

Appendix 1

Having opened it,Click on sign up to get started

For instance, you can type... as a Digital creator;help me generate a mission statement of about 100 words (Replace 'Digital creator with your brand name.)Or   as a Digital creator,help me generate a catchy slogan for my brand

You can craft your command prompt Depending on what you want AI to Help you do

Note: you can use this AI to create any Content of your choice using the command prompt, anything you ask it to do, it will definitely help you do it with ease, you don't need to pay anyone for contents,this method has helped a lot of Brand owners and Digital Entrepreneurs. Please; check recommended resources/ tools at the last Page and take it very serious it's another way of rewarding you for your time and decision to read this book

To learn more practical ways of giving chatgpt the right prompt Check here

To learn how to create an online presence using about.com You Can Check Here

To learn Facebook Professional Mode
<u>Kindly Check Here</u>

Next is!

1. Choosing the look of your **Brand** (colors and font)

2. Design your **logo**

Apply your branding across your business and evolve it as you grow.

Congratulations! you have successfully created your brand with ease!Now that you have clearly defined your brand, what next?

- ***Adjust Your Image to Your Convictions:***

So how do you gain brand belief in the first place?

Crafting compelling brand narratives serves as the foundation for building brand trust. Instead of relying solely on promotional content, engaging in emotional storytelling that aligns with your target audience's worldview is crucial. These narratives, not centered on product features, but rather on evoking emotions, contribute to the establishment of a genuine connection. Aligning your brand with your values involves ensuring that your business practices reflect your principles, fostering authenticity.

Authenticity is paramount. When your brand aligns with your beliefs, authenticity emerges, fostering trust among customers who can discern sincerity. It goes beyond mere verbal declarations; it's about embodying these values in your actions. Consistency is key; your beliefs should permeate all facets of your brand, reinforcing your message and building a reliable identity.

Attracting like-minded customers becomes a natural outcome when your brand resonates with shared values.

This connection can foster a strong community around your brand, nurturing loyalty and advocacy. Employee engagement is enhanced when your team shares these principles, creating a positive workplace culture.

Moreover, brands with enduring success often have a deeper purpose beyond profit. When driven by genuine beliefs, a brand is better equipped to navigate challenges and adapt to evolving environments, ensuring long-term success.

One may ask what even is brand belief ?

Brand belief manifests when customers invest unwavering trust in a brand, abstaining from comparing it to others. These devoted customers transform into brand ambassadors, extolling the virtues of the brand and willingly purchasing new releases at premium price points

Typically, individuals with brand beliefs integrate their perception of the brand with their lifestyle, values, and personality, viewing the brand as a reflection of their self-importance.

Customers in this category may swiftly disassociate from a brand if its actions jeopardize their perceived values, making brands vulnerable to reputational damage. For brands relying on such devoted customer segments, caution is necessary when altering core values or supporting causes incongruent with the original principles.

Prominent examples of brands enjoying brand belief include Nike and Apple. Nike customers display brand loyalty by consistently acquiring the latest releases, even if they possess a collection of unworn trainers. Similarly, Apple enthusiasts eagerly await new iPhone releases, upgrading annually despite their phones being in optimal condition. Apple's brand belief, however, has reportedly waned post-Steve Jobs, attributed to perceived innovation stagnation and inconsistent pricing strategies.

Establishing brand belief surpasses having superior products; it necessitates cultivating a perception that aligns with the audience's worldview. This process demands meticulous planning and a laser-focused approach. Sustaining brand belief involves strategic social media marketing, where a robust messaging strategy aligned with core values serves as a guide to prevent straying from the path that initially cultivated brand belief.

- ***Utilize the Story Brand Idea to Change Your Organization Culture***

By simply changing your brand's message, you could potentially transform your company's culture. This book dives into the significant effect of StoryBrand on reshaping an organization's way of life from the inside.

Beyond the stereotypical images of cheerful workers, festive office gatherings, and free snacks in the break room, defining a company's culture requires more than just those things. The Public Organization of Free Business appropriately portrays it as "the manner in which we get things done around here." While each organization has an exceptional culture, not all are positive, and uncontrolled, it can empty the imperativeness from an association. Studies emphasize the detrimental effects of disengagement, such as absenteeism, injuries, reckless spending, and even resignations, as well as the crucial role that employee engagement plays in business success.

Organization pioneers bear the obligation of guaranteeing their organization's way of life is decidedly the association. Using StoryBrand, pioneers can start an extraordinary change in culture, influencing change from the center. Understanding organization culture requires perceiving that even in the littlest groups, a culture normally arises as people, impacted by private encounters and values, add to an aggregate objective. Whether deliberately or unwittingly, individuals imbue their extraordinary foundation into the associations they join.

Consider in the event that your organization brings out a feeling of fellowship likened to a day camp as opposed to a conventional business setting. Provided that this is true, congrats, as you've developed a culture that encourages a local area feel.

Progressing to a conversation about your image, Brené Earthy colored understanding sounds valid: " Your organization image is what others say regarding you when you're not in the room." This supports that a convincing brand message is essential in forming discernments both inside and remotely.

Model #1: A gathering of companions is hanging out, discussing how they'd never purchase their blossoms from anyplace yet Nearby Bloom Shop on the grounds that the staff is so well disposed there. The organization has developed an extraordinary organization brand and client commitment locally.

Model #2: Among companions, there's an agreement that they purposely try not to drive past Cook and Crumbler Bread kitchen because of their unequivocally hated organization logo, discoloring the bread shop's standing inside the local area and among expected clients. It is emphasized that a brand includes more than just a logo and interactions between employees; it includes the whole client experience, molding the character of the brand.

Adjusting organization culture with the brand is vital, as a positive culture can decidedly impact the brand. On the other hand, a negative reputation that extends beyond the workplace can result from a toxic work environment. At the point when an organization's way of life and brand are as one, it makes a positive far reaching influence. Leaders who truly care about the culture of their company employ branding strategies that are in line with their cultural objectives. This has an effect on employee behavior and customer perceptions.

The collaboration of organization culture and brand is depicted as a delightful arrangement, making a mutually beneficial arrangement for representatives and clients the same.

The idea of transforming a brand into a convincing story is presented, compared to adding a sprinkle of pixie residue to the brand's story. It underscores the significance of making a spellbinding air around the brand, making it an experience for all interested parties.

The notice of utilizing another person's story as an illustration is noted, with a commitment that the decision will turn out to be clear as the conversation advances. This approach means to explain key experiences connected with narrating and marking in the resulting areas.

Master the Keys to Being Seen, Heard, and Understood;

Imagine yourself as the primary follow up on a phase. Dominating the keys implies turning into the main event, the one everybody's humming about. Being seen is about not mixing away from plain sight but rather standing apart like a spotlight is on you. Being heard is having a voice that slices through the clamor, making individuals need to tune in. And comprehending? Indeed, that is tied in with communicating in a language that everybody gets, framing an association that goes beyond anything that can be put into words. Like having these mystical keys make the way for being a brand that orders consideration, impacts others, and is perfectly clear in its message.

Ways of feeling seen heard and comprehended

#1. *Consider yourself responsible for self-improvement.*
You show fortitude with the group when you openly work to improve as a pioneer.
Look for input.
Make yourself vulnerable. Proclaim improvement objectives.
Discuss advancement. Tell individuals how you're doing.
Hope for something else of yourself than you anticipate from others.
#2. *Give clear assumptions.* Everybody has to understand what achievement resembles before they go to work today. Improvement opens doors associated with accomplishment.
Individuals feel seen, heard, and comprehended when you assist them with rising.
Put the top strengths of each team member on the wall. An illustration of a conference room
#3. *Perceive qualities openly.* Everybody in the group has to know the best five qualities of everybody in the group. A few groups post each other's assets on the gathering room wall.

#4. *Plan formative one-on-ones.* Where would you like to go? What might we do for you to arrive?

Gallup's examination shows high-advancement societies add to feeling seen, heard, and comprehended.

#5. *Figure out how to tune in.*

In the event that you believe you're a decent audience you're most likely off-base.

When people are speaking, look at them.

Quit squirming.

Make inquiries.

Restate.

Thank individuals for contributing.

You can tune in without resolving to do all that individuals say.

#6. *Acknowledge the human condition*. Even if you possess weaknesses.

Individuals feel seen, heard, and comprehended when you know their shortcomings and regard their commitment.

#7. *Develop empathy*. Say, "It seems like you feel _________." When you are off, ask yourself, "What am I missing?"

Assert individuals' energy. " What's going on for you right now? You just lit up.
"An individual begins to live when he can live beyond himself." Albert,

What to learn from this section

- *Turn your brand into a beacon of trust and loyalty.*
- *Learn the art of crafting compelling narratives, fostering authenticity, and aligning with values. Dive into the power of StoryBrand to reshape your organizational culture.*
- *Take the first step towards enduring success*
- *If you Act now, you will revolutionize how your brand connects, resonates, and thrives in the evolving landscape."*
- *cultivate brand belief and engage your audience strategically.*
- *Ready to redefine your brand narrative? Start now."*

Key Number Three

understand where your Listeners might be coming from

You might have heard the expression "understand where your listeners might be coming from" a considerable amount, yet on the off chance that everybody really comprehends the importance, many bombed organizations could in any case be near.

Your business' items can be remarkable and even life-changing, yet in the event that your crowd doesn't realize they exist, you'll not have anything to show for your endeavors with the exception of sitting around idly and cash. So, how can you guarantee that your products will be recognized?

•*Comprehend Your Crowd's Longings and Center your Message*

Understanding your audience is the first step. Whenever you've demonstrated that, you can sort out how to get inside the head of expected clients to comprehend their necessities and wants completely. Suppose you've done whatever it may take to recognize your interest group yet are uncertain the way in which you can contact them. Learn to expect the unexpected. Additional time and cash squandered.

This guide will take you through the course of why "understanding your listeners' perspective" and understanding how to contact your crowd will assist with sending that astounding and novel result of yours taking off the racks.

Okay, envision you're facilitating a gathering, and your visitors are your crowd. Presently, you would rather not serve pizza assuming everybody's desire for burgers, isn't that so? It is a piece like that to Grasp your crowd. It's tied in with understanding what they need, what really matters to them. Learn about their desires and what truly excites them by delving into their world and conversing with them. It wouldn't fret perusing; it's more similar to being a decent audience at the party, checking out their center message. Thus, when you comprehend what they're about, you can fit your image to be the ideal party, serving up precisely the exact thing they pine for.

For what reason is it important to recognize your interest group?

If you have any desire to move stock, draw in with clients, and support an effective business, you really want to realize who you're focusing on and sort out a method for telling them you exist.

As you might have heard, "quality written substance is the final deciding factor." Like an extraordinary item, excellent substance showcasing will draw in expected clients. Content plays a

basic job in your promoting system, yet you should understand who your listeners' perspective is before your pen raises a ruckus around town or rather, before your fingers hit the keys whether it's for virtual entertainment, your site, an item depiction, your blog, or any showcasing materials. What's the point of posting content if nobody sees it? It might appear to be a simple idea to execute, yet 80% of brand made content neglected to convey significant shopper commitment in 2021

You should likewise know your own image and have the option to respond to these inquiries:

For what reason should your interest group care about your administrations or items?

What are your item's advantages from the purchaser's perspective?

What is your Exceptional Selling Suggestion

How are your rivals showcasing their items effectively?

Numerous organizations become so centered around selling their items that they neglect to require some investment to comprehend what arrangement they're conveying to customers. Using demographics to identify your target audience will narrow it down from everyone in the world to just those who would benefit from your product. This information also provides valuable content for marketing messages. The following are some typical demographics to think about:

Gender, race, marital status, education level, location, and income level: By studying demographics, you can identify a group of people who are most interested in your products and services. For instance, in the event that you're selling ladies' clothing, you would resolve where they're investing their energy to contact them. Females overall are a huge crowd, so the initial step is reducing your pursuit. Maybe your attire line is equipped towards mature ladies with enough discretionary cash flow to spend on excellent things. These ladies might be aged 50-70, with normal earnings of $100,000-$150,000. Now that you've laid out your crowd's socioeconomics, you can utilize that data to direct your promoting channel decisions.

All things considered, don't stop with just socioeconomics. You ought to likewise invest energy on a crowd of people examining your clients' psychographics, which centers around ways of behaving. (DigitalDoughnut.com) gives instances of habitually utilized psychographics, including:

Values

Character and mentalities

Interests and leisure activities

Data utilization propensities

Buying propensities

Utilizing this strong data, you can then make (purchaser personas.com) that address your optimal clients. Such examination based profiles assist you with getting inside your clients' heads, permitting you to all the more likely figure out their requirements and agony. This comprehension is essential for establishing trust, which results in sales.

Communicating genuine understanding and concern for your customers is the best way to build trust. Making purchaser personas to direct your showcasing technique will assist you with staying zeroed in on your clients' necessities.

Furnished with the meaning of your main interest group (and their ways of behaving and problem areas), you can move to your following stage: creating high-quality content that will captivate your audience. for every purchaser persona and promote on various channels.

Distinguish and Verbalize the Issues Your Crowd Appearances

Consider your crowd companions who come to you for counsel. Presently, they could have a few difficulties, isn't that so? Recognizing and articulating the issues your crowd faces resembles being that wise companion who listens to them as well as assists them with tracking down arrangements. It's tied in with understanding their battles, the barricades they experience, and afterward being the hero with the responses. At the point when you can pinpoint their concerns and communicate in their language, you become the go-to companion they trust. In this way, it's not just about talking; Being that trustworthy friend who understands them and having a meaningful conversation are the keys.

Use social media demographics and psychographics to find the right communication platform to effectively reach your new audience, especially on social media. Go to considerable lengths to keep up to date with insights and patterns as they change, as clients are fussy and can forsake a platform.

(Campaignmonitor.com) summarizes it perfectly: " By distinguishing where your crowd hangs out on the web and limiting that crowd down into interesting gatherings, you can give the absolute most pertinent substance and associate with individuals who need to understand what you bring to the table." Boom! Socioeconomics will assist you with finding where your ideal interest group invests their energy. You might have heard the expression "understand what your listeners might be thinking" a considerable amount, however in the event that everybody really comprehended the significance, many bombed organizations could in any case be near.

Your business' items can be novel and even life-changing, yet on the off chance that your crowd doesn't realize they exist, you'll not have anything to show for your endeavors aside from sitting around and cash. So how would you guarantee your products gain the appreciation they merit?

To begin with, you really want to comprehend who your crowd is. Whenever you've demonstrated that, you can sort out how to get inside the head of likely clients to comprehend their necessities and wants completely. Suppose you've done whatever it takes to recognize your interest group yet are uncertain the way that you can contact them. Learn to expect the unexpected. Additional time and cash squandered.

This guide will take you through the course of why "understanding where your listeners might be coming from" and understanding how to contact your crowd will assist with sending that astonishing and extraordinary result of yours taking off the racks.

Draw in your main interest group through advertising correspondences.

It is essential to keep in mind that even though your demographics may be similar to those of your clients, this does not necessarily mean that you are an accurate representation of your intended audience. Nancy Marshall puts it: "Distinguishing the right segment requires a comprehensive perspective on everyone." Try not to expect that in light of the fact that a showcasing strategy or message would deal with you, it will resound with your ideal interest group.

Exploring socio economics will deliver profits

To contact your recently discovered crowd successfully particularly via online entertainment utilize virtual entertainment socioeconomics and psychographics as your manual for tracking down the right correspondence stage. Go to considerable lengths to keep up to date with insights and patterns as they change, as clients are fussy and can forsake a stage as a group.

For instance, Facebook used to be the sole virtual entertainment stage for recent college grads; presently it's undeniably more famous with more established socioeconomics.

This capacity to answer clients is basic since commitment is everything in the realm of advertising. North of 2 billion shoppers use SMS, Whatsapp, or Facebook Courier consistently to visit, and they are 5x bound to answer these talk channels than to email

(Chat baby, ManyChat, Chat Node, Drift) is an automation system that effectively coordinates chatbots into your computerized promoting methodology. You can use it to control north of 1 billion discussions overall consistently

The most effective way to get to "understand where your listeners might be coming from" so you can give answers for their concerns is to exploit the many wellsprings of information accessible. You can learn about your customers, where to find them online, and how to engage with them by utilizing tools like ManyChat and demographics, psychographics, and other data.

With this data close by, you can support devotion and increment deals to move your business along solid for a really long time!

Key Number Four

Present your item or administration as the Solution.

What issue does your item or your brand settle?

The most effective way to figure out what issue your item or administration settles for your clients is by asking them!

While acquainting your image , guarantee to ask your crowd "what might I do".

Begin asking your crowd "what issue would you say you are encountering that I can assist you with addressing?"

What offers you superpowers by taking action at these responses is that you can utilize your client's genuine words while characterizing issues. Not got any clients to inquire? Go to Amazon, select a product that falls into your service or product category, and then read the customer reviews! Or then again attempt (TrustPilot, Google analytics,and hotspot CRM) to understand surveys.

Search for

Repeatable words, expressions or ideas

What issues are focused on over others?

At the point when you've found the issue you can settle for your clients (in a way that would sound natural to them), take a stab at penetrating down a piece further.

Recognize the issue. Furthermore, ask yourself "so what?" For what reason is this issue? What does this issue resemble in their life? How does this issue cause them to feel?

This assists you with figuring out why this is an issue or its results being an issue.

Focus on the positive Involve people in the conversation you're having with them, whether it's via email, sales page, social media post, or discovery call, by focusing on their dreams and goals. Show them what is (everything being equal) conceivable. Flip the issue into the arrangement and utilize this to catch their eye and trigger their interest.

- ***Tailor your brand message to resonate with your crowd.***

Having explored their requirements, wants, trouble spots, and goals. Tailor your messages to address their particular difficulties and proposition arrangements that talk straightforwardly to their souls and psyches.

When you have an unmistakable image of your crowd, you can make a message that impacts them.

Utilize the Right Language: To interface with your crowd, you really want to communicate in their language. Utilize the words, expressions, and phrasing that they use. Keep away from language, popular expressions, or specialized terms that could befuddle or estrange them.

Highlight the Benefits: Your crowd is more intrigued by how your item or administration can help them, as opposed to its highlights. In this way, center around the advantages of your contribution, and how it can tackle their concerns or improve their lives.

Utilize Social Evidence: When a brand has social proof, people are more likely to trust it and make a purchase. This can come as client tributes, contextual analyses, surveys, or support from forces to be reckoned with or specialists in your industry.

Show Sympathy; Sympathy is the capacity to comprehend and talk about the thoughts of others. By showing compassion, you can fabricate an association with your crowd and show them that you care about their necessities and concerns. Show how your product or service has helped other people by telling stories or sharing personal stories.

Make Your Message Unique: The process of adapting your message to an individual's particular requirements or preferences is known as personalization. Use information and examination to fragment your crowd and convey designated messages in light of their way of behaving, interests, or socioeconomics.

Get the issue

Whenever you've shown them their fantasy can turn into a reality momentarily let them know you get it. You grasp the issue. Whether this is on the grounds that you've been there and done it, or you've assisted many individuals with that issue. Also, you know how life resembled for them when they were encountering the issue.

Now is the time to demonstrate the answer.

A large number of my clients are incredible at showing their clients current realities about what they do that takes care of the issue. What they miss are the personal arrangements they bring. Let individuals know how they feel when they don't have the issue any longer. How does that connect with the substantial highlights of the help or item you're introducing as the arrangement?

What next!

Presently you know the issue your item or administration addresses for your clients, you can consolidate it in the entirety of your advertising brands.

Key Number Five

Be Intentional Online

Create a professional online presence with a personal website and active social media profiles.

Influence the Force of Online Entertainment: Your digital presence can be built and maintained effectively using social media platforms. Distinguish the stages that reverberate with your interest group the most and center your endeavors there. Whether it's Instagram, Twitter, LinkedIn, or TikTok, keep a functioning presence by sharing a blend of unique substance, organized articles, and drawing in visuals. Draw in with your crowd by answering remarks, partaking in conversations, and in any event, teaming up with powerhouses. Online entertainment is a two-way road, so make sure to tune in and collaborate however much you broadcast.

Establish a personal website and active social media profiles to establish a professional online Okay! how about we separate it in straightforward terms:

(BONUS 2)

- ***Step 1***: Set Up Your Own Site by Picking a Phase: choose aboutme.com or a web designer like Squarespace, WordPress, or

Wix. There you can make your site without knowing bewildered code. Additionally, it is suitable for novices.

•*Make Your Area:* Your space resembles your internet based address like www.yourname.com pick something straightforward and simple to recall. Most web designers permit you to buy a space through them.

Make sure the domain name reflects who you are; I recommend using your brand name.

- *Create Your Pages:* Consider your site a computerized continuation. You'll need pages like "*About Me*", "*Resume*," and perhaps a "*Portfolio*" on the off chance that you have work to feature. Compose a smidgen about yourself and your excursion.

- ***Add Contact Data:*** Make it simple for individuals to reach out. Make a "Contact" page with your email or a contact structure. To sort out some way to do it for nothing

(Go to the bonus page and click on the link to learn or use the Url link to search for it)

- ***Exhibit Your Image:*** Add an individual touch - use tones, text styles, and visuals that impact you. Allow guests to discover what your identity is.

I have a reward for you here, Previously or subsequent to making your site, guarantee your image name is enrolled on Google, this way you can help your perceivability and validity and finding you wouldn't be troublesome

How would you do this?

- Sign into the email account you want to use for your business profile, go to your search area, type google.com/bussiness and search

- Scroll down to where you will see Google business profile
- Click on get listed on Google
- Click on business profile
- Then, Click on manage now, follow the instructions to start building your brand on Google, Remember to choose Your Platforms Carefully When Setting Up Your Social Media Profiles: Try not to overpower yourself. Begin with a couple of stages that line up with your objectives. Eg; LinkedIn is incredible for proficient associations, while Instagram, Facebook or Twitter could suit innovative undertakings.

Step 2: Steady Profile Pictures: Utilize a similar profile picture across all stages. People will be able to easily identify you as this.

Create a Bio: Compose a short, captivating bio. Notice what you do, your inclinations, and why individuals should interface with you. Add your site interface if conceivable.

Share Customary Updates: Post consistently about things you're energetic about or projects you're chipping away at. Let your personality shine through by being yourself.

Step 3: Draw in and Associate with Others: Follow individuals in your industry or those with comparative interests. Draw in with their posts by remarking and sharing.

Be Receptive: At the point when individuals remark or message you, answer expeditiously. This demonstrates your proactive and approachable nature.

Share Important Substance: Share about your image as well as fascinating substance. This positions you as somebody with significant experiences.

Step 4: Keep it Proficient; I will give YouTube connect on how you can transform your Facebook profile into proficient account ,to learn go to the page and click on the link for the YouTube guide or use the Url link to search for it

Mind Your Language: Keep your language expert and positive. Stay away from oversharing individual subtleties that probably won't be pertinent to your image.

Actually take a look at Security Settings: Survey and change protection settings on your virtual entertainment stages to control who sees what. ***Always Update:*** Keep your site and social profiles exceptional. Add new achievements or projects and remove any information that is out of date. Keep in mind, your web-based presence is an impression of you, so make it veritable and pleasant for others to interface with.

Advance Your Site and Search engine optimization: Your site fills in as your computerized base camp. It's where expected clients or devotees get a complete perspective on what your identity is and what you offer. Make sure your website is mobile-friendly, easy to use, and visually appealing. Moreover, put resources into site improvement (Web optimization) to work on your site's perceivability on web indexes. Lead catchphrase examination to distinguish the terms your crowd is looking for, and integrate them normally into your substance. Superior grade, applicable backlinks from respectable sources can likewise upgrade your site's position and lift its web index rankings.

Connect Through Email Advertising: Even though social media is important, email marketing is still a great way to connect with your audience directly. Urge guests to your site and virtual entertainment stages to buy into your email list. Convey normal pamphlets that offer some benefit, like restrictive substance, industry experiences, and extraordinary offers. Personalization is key in email promotion, so section your rundown and design your messages to explicit gatherings in view of their inclinations and ways of behaving. A drawing in an educational email can direct people to your site and keep your crowd associated and informed.

Embrace Visual Marking: A solid visual brand is vital and separates you from the group. Consistency in your visuals, for example, logos, variety plans, and typography, assists work with marking acknowledgment. Your unique personality and business values should be reflected in your visual identity, which should resonate with your target audience. Share visually appealing graphics and videos across your digital platforms that are in line with the message of your brand. Visual substance is bound to be shared and can altogether build your web-based reach.

Key Number Six

Communicate Transformation

Since you have online presence we should discuss how you can win more crowd by utilizing your virtual entertainment to Show the positive change your clients experienced while associating with your image your brand

Ponder when you had a striking involvement in a business. You may not recollect everything but you most likely recall the good sentiments around the item you got, Presently, recollect a negative encounter you had. Maybe you felt baffled or as though you were dealt with unreasonably.

Did you compose a survey or enlighten somebody concerning the experience? In the two situations, these feelings frequently drive individuals to impart their experience to other people, whether essentially or through verbal. They inspire us to encourage others to share our happiness or avoid making mistakes. In the event that you're a business chief in any industry, you know that making supportive, connecting with, and frictionless encounters for your clients can emphatically influence the view of your image, increment buys, and make steadfast fans forever.

The reasons why business leaders need to concentrate on the customer experience in order to ensure ongoing growth and engagement are outlined below. There are a number of ways to enhance the experience of your customers.

What Is Client Experience?

Customer experience, or CX, is how a customer feels about your brand and interacts with it. Any time a client has some sort of touchpoint with your image, it's additional to the assortment of encounters that makes up their impression of your image. Basically, if you have enough good interactions with them, they'll be happy enough to keep coming back; If they have enough bad experiences, they might never think of you again.

The following are a portion of the sorts of encounters a client can have with a business:

A client ventures into a retail location and is welcomed by a well disposed specialist proposing to assist them with tracking down an item.

A client follows a business via virtual entertainment, and preferences a post that shows them a novel, new thing.

A client needs to pay for an item, yet remains in line for 15 minutes in light of the fact that only one clerk is working while the others visit among themselves.

A client visits a business' site and can without much of a stretch find out about the administrations the business offers.

A client calls a business' administration line however is dealt with inconsiderately and doesn't get their inquiry settled.

A customer returns to a favorite establishment because they enjoy the ambience.

Encounters regularly are not nonpartisan. Clients will feel either emphatically or adversely about a touchpoint, and that inclination and feeling can influence the amount they'll enjoy with you or how steadfast they'll be, today and into what's to come. Fortunately business pioneers have some control over what sorts of encounters their clients have. However, why is zeroing in on encounters so important?

Why are customer experiences so important?

Client experience can represent the deciding moment of your business. It's not just about whether they get the items and administrations they're chasing; Reinforcing your brand's value and securing future customers are also important considerations.Investing in the customer experience is crucial for the following reasons:

Encounters matter as much as items and administrations. There's higher maintenance for fulfilled clients, Positive experiences result in contented customers, and 90% of those who are highly satisfied with a brand say they are very likely to make additional purchases from that brand.

Encounters influence income: As 84% of businesses that improved their customer experiences saw an increase in revenue, brands that place a high value on providing excellent experiences to their customers will benefit financially.

Experience will command a premium from customers. Assuming you offer your clients extraordinary encounters, they're more able to pay something else for your items and administrations as much as 18% more.

Negative encounters have an effect, as well,

The encounters that you make for your clients straightforwardly influence the way they take from learning about your image to turning into a long lasting fan. You can utilize encounters to additional upgrade and drive their excursion in the accompanying ways.

Client Awareness: The initial step on the client venture is acquiring consciousness of your items, administrations, and brand, like catching wind of the brand from companions, or perusing a positive survey. This implies that they catch wind of your image from the positive encounters others have proactively had.

As we referenced, the main explanation one looks towards your site is that *they're searching for an answer for an issue.* Many organizations are committing this error that they don't discuss the issue they address. Remember that arrangements don't just exist. There is a purpose for its presence. Indeed, in light of the fact that an answer without an issue is of no importance.

In addition, when you notice about the issue your administration or item settles, it has a setting. Also, just along these lines, your clients bond with you. They may think:

"Amazing! At last, somebody understands what I need! Lastly, somebody understands what I'm going through! Somebody grasps my concern, so they should have an answer for it."

Your clients interface with you and trust you to take care of their concerns when you discuss the issue your clients are living with and search for an answer.

Consideration: A customer is more likely to make a purchase from you if they start to feel good about their interactions with your brand after a few times. Nonetheless, on the off chance that a client has a negative encounter the site is too difficult to even consider exploring, they can't track down somebody in that frame of mind to respond to their inquiries they're probably going to leave their thought of your image by and large.

Purchase: certain encounters with a brand will build their certainty that you're the one they need to give their cash to and will make a buy.

Retention: Brands have the opportunity to re-engage their customers in new ways that provide value and increase their willingness to continue buying after the initial purchase to continue providing positive experiences to their customers.

Loyalty: The final destination is long-term customer loyalty and retention. At this stage, customers feel positively enough about your brand to be a fan and evangelist, but this can only happen if you continue to provide positive experiences that reinforce their positive feelings about you.

the character in a story that helps the hero win the day. So, this is the responsibility of brands and leaders to be Guides. And, being in that position, it is our responsibility to help our customers win the day.

And, this is where your products & services come in. It could be said that they're like Batman's utility belt. It provides him with the tools he needs to win the day and those that make him a hero. Likewise, your consumers or users already consider that they are the only heroes. But still, there is one thing that they don't do, that is if you know what they're going through.

Don't forget that almost every hero has a deep desire, like something they want. But some problems for sure are getting in their way, which are preventing them from getting what they want.

So, this is the reason why they're on your website. Yes, all they are doing is looking for a solution. Hence try to reach their hearts by telling them what they're going through and how you can help them.

Business leaders who want to create great experiences for their customers need to be deliberate about doing so. If you're embarking upon creating a customer experience strategy or want to improve your current approach, here's where to start.

Conceptualize Your Customer Experience Strategy

Start developing or improving your customer experiences by first creating a strategy or vision for how you want to impact the customer journey. For example, if your website has a high bounce rate or abandoned cart rate, overhaul your website experience. If your in-store purchases have dropped off, look at ways to increase foot traffic by improving customer service, offering more in-store technology, or streamlining the checkout process.

As you plan your strategy, ask yourself what experiences you could create that:

- aligns with your brand and serves your target audience or customer base.
- Make the customer journey more efficient and frictionless,
- create more convenience
- provide more friendly and knowledge service
- make paying for products quick and painless

Be sure to include in your strategy what success looks like for you, and how you'll go about measuring success after a rollout. Create clear objectives of what you want to accomplish, like more purchases, higher dollar amount per purchase, or more time spent on the website. Then, identify Key Performance Indicators, or KPIs, that you can track so you can determine if you hit your goals.

Finally, as you evaluate your overall customer experience approach, consider creating an executive role like a Customer Experience Officer (CXO) who could lead the creation, implementation, delivery, and measurement of your customer experiences.

Implement Your New or Improved Customer Experiences

Now that you've determined the types of experiences that will serve your customers and add value to their journey, implement them.

First, start small. If you want to implement augmented reality in your in-store locations, don't roll it out across all locations at once, but pilot it in one location to learn how it will work and if customers are responsive.

Educate customers on new experiences as well. If you're implementing new self-service ordering screens, have associates invite customers over to the screens and teach them how to use it.

Don't forget to promote your new experiences across your marketing channels so that customers can get excited about the experience before they try it.

Finally, have a system in place for tracking data and customer feedback around your new experiences so that you can gauge their impact, and use Customer Relationship Manager (CRM) software to track customer touch points.

Analyze Your KPI Data to Determine How Your Experiences Affect Your Business Now is the Time to Determine How Your Experiences

Affect Your Business Maybe you patched up your site for a superior client experience, and found that your neglected truck rate went down and buys went up accomplishing one of your objectives. Or on the other hand, assuming your information shows no change after your site patch up, you realize that you really want to examine what else should be changed to hit your objective.

There are various measurements you can use to follow the progress of the encounters you make for your clients, which can include:

NPS: The Net Advertiser Score (NPS) just poses one inquiry: " How probably could you prescribe this organization to a companion?" Positive encounters lead to cheerful clients who need to tell others, and organizations can follow that through their NPS.

Client consistency standard: This measurement tells you at what rate you're keeping clients, and who is proceeding to draw in with your image. Customers who continue to value your goods, services, and experiences are said to have a high retention rate.

Client stir rate: This measurement tells you at what rate you're losing clients. This can help you figure out how and where engagement is falling, as well as whether customers are leaving because of your experiences.

LTV: You can find out how much a customer has spent on your product or service over the course of their relationship with your company by using the customer lifetime value (LTV or CLV). In the event that LTV increments, you realize you have a reliable client able to keep buying with you.

Measurements intended for your encounters: At long last, track measurements that will be affected by your encounters. For instance, assuming you carry out an in-store experience that directs people to your site, track site visits, skip rate, time on page, and everyday guests. Track those numbers with your POS data if your experiences revolve around increasing the amount per purchase.

Position your customer as the hero, emphasizing their challenges and aspirations.

Step by step instructions to Make the Client the Legend of Your Story

A typical misstep organizations put forth in showcasing attempts is situating their image as the legend of the story. You might need to wear the cape, drive the Batmobile, and kick the bad guy's butt (and who could fault you?), yet, most brands neglect the interests of clients when they center themselves.

The unforgiving truth is that your clients couldn't care less about your organization or items - their consideration is about how you'll address their issues. Assuming that you believe your clients should purchase your items or administrations, your advertising ought to rotate around your client and their difficulties.

At the point when your client plays the featured job in your showcasing endeavors, they feel appreciated and are bound to download your substance, follow you via virtual entertainment, finish up a contact structure, and (you got it!) Research has shown that client driven organizations are 60% more productive than organizations that don't zero in on the client. On a similar note, McKinsey viewed that as 70% of purchasing encounters depend on how the client feels they have been dealt with.

In any case, fabricating a client driven mentality will not work out more or less by accident. Before you execute a fruitful client driven promoting methodology, you really want to acquire a more profound comprehension of being genuinely client centered.

What is a client driven organization?

Priorities straight, what does it try and intend to be a client driven organization? It's not just about offering outstanding client support; it likewise implies helping the client through each phase of the purchaser's excursion, from the mindfulness and exploring stage to the last phases of direction and, surprisingly, after their buy is finished. A client driven organization teaches their clients and assists them with settling on an informed purchasing choice.

At the point when you focus on client centricity, you're putting the client at the focal point of every one of your choices and key preparation. You're making a positive client experience by zeroing in on their necessities more than your overall revenues. Your main concern ought to make their lives more straightforward by responding to their consuming inquiries, giving instructive substance or proposing a particular arrangement whenever they've demonstrated they're prepared and open for suggestions.

An incredible illustration of a client driven organization is Amazon. By developing products and making decisions based on their customers' needs and wants, Amazon consistently delights their customer base. While client surveys are on essentially every site these days, Amazon was quick to show these audits. Amazon President,

Jeff Bezos, needed to accomplish something beyond selling items; He wanted to "help customers make decisions about their purchases."

Apple is another company that shows a strategy that is focused on the customer. Apple really models their client assistance highlights after the cordiality business; Genius Bar is like the concierge. Apple is continually on top of addressing their clients' requirements. In fact, they respond to customers' emails directly; Even CEO Tim Cook has stated that he personally responds to emails every day. They let their clients in on that they are valued by blowing away standard assumptions for client care.

Companies that focus on the needs of their customers are there when they need them, not just when it's convenient for them. They furnish their clients with data and admittance to items or records day in and day out. USAA, for example, was quick to make an application that would permit their clients to put aside installments by means of their iPhone and furthermore to send refreshes on account adjustments through instant message. They engage clients to get opportune updates on their funds, and, hence, further develop consumer loyalty.

How would you become a client driven Brand

Before you can make the client the legend of your story, you want to put yourself from their perspective. That's what to do, you should realize whose shoes you're venturing into. Investigate your current client base by conveying studies or checking famous web-based entertainment stages.

At the point when your ideal clients find content covering subjects they're really inspired by, they're bound to impart it to collaborators and companions, spread the news about your organization, and return for more.

Permit Investment from Clients

There could be no more excellent method for making a client driven culture than permitting your clients to partake in your image's story or mission effectively. For instance, when the blockbuster film "The Issue in Our Stars" turned out in theaters, the maker Atlantic Records gathered in excess of 3,800 bits of fan photographs north of 3 days through #TFIOSencouragements on Instagram. They then assembled these photographs in a web-based exhibition where fans could view, offer, and decide in favor of their top picks.

In this situation, the creation group set their possible clients at the center of attention while likewise sharing their significant substance. They created a positive customer experience by making their fans and movie ticket purchasers feel special, even if it's only for a brief moment.

Furthermore, the Client Makes all the difference...Getting every one of the above rehearses either way will permit you to make and execute a fruitful client driven promoting methodology. You are demonstrating to the customer that you are worthy of their time by taking these proactive steps toward becoming a customer-centric business or brand. At the point when you understand every one of the necessities, needs, and inclinations of your client and use them to shape your advertising endeavors, you are guaranteeing that all your business choices rotate around the client. At this point when the client knows you are not just about their viewpoints and concerns yet additionally that you use them to drive your essential preparation, they are bound to get back to your organization for more data and to make a buy. When a product is made to solve their specific problem, a piece of content answers their questions, and social media posts address their interests, they will feel appreciated and understood.

First and foremost, you must demonstrate that you care about your customers if you want them to care about you. Making your clients the focal point of your image's universe will assist you with fostering a reliable following and find new business potential open doors. They'll be the legend of your advertising technique, yet you'll realize that your organization or item made it workable for them to make all the difference.

Individuals will interface with you and trust you to assist them with taking care of their concerns just when they will see that you comprehend their most profound cravings as if they're just looking for an answer for their concern.

Build emotional connections through storytelling.

The first thing that comes to mind is emotion. Associate with your clients/clients inwardly. Indeed, to construct enduring relations with your clients, you really want to fabricate a close to home associate m. that doesn't mean you want to make the individual bond or something with your clients, yet this implies that you ought to be proficient with them like reliable about the conveyance timing, consistently accessible for a discussion, continue to refresh the improvement condition of items, be in the discipline about the whole cycle, and so on. Well, these parameters strengthen the relationship with the client. What's more, along these lines, they keep in touch with you for a more extended run. Many organizations have a few clients like until the end of time. This indicates that businesses form such strong bonds with their customers that a single customer becomes a repeat customer.

Additionally, we speculate that we all have the same goal. However, this is the current obstacle, and in order to overcome it, you must emotionally connect with your clients. narrating isn't restricted to books or getting kids into bed around evening time. Composing a story and building a profound association with your clients is one of the best ways of building a dependable relationship and guarantee that your clients return again and again, and think about your business as their best option in the entirety of their requirements. The accompanying five stages help to make stories that make you vital and interesting to clients. One of the most efficient methods for establishing a long-term relationship with your clients and ensuring that they will continue to use your company for all of their needs is to tell a story and create an emotional connection with them.

Below are the accompanying five stages that help you to make stories that are critical and interesting to clients.

While you're attempting to sell somebody, make it individual and uncover what it has meant for one individual's life, or the way that it had such an effect on how one individual gets past the day. A good Example of that is the link I provided to you as a guide in the bonus page, it's actually my clients page, This is quite a lot more engaging and compelling than attempting to mass-market a thing - as that is a strategy that individuals are for the most part tired of. For instance, humor might be more interesting to certain clients in a business, while nostalgia might be more interesting to other people. These locales can assist you with making a brand persona that can in a split second associate with your possible future clients.

At the point when you make a persona and a story that is interesting to your clients, you shouldn't simply make them a unique case. Give them a bend, and ensure the narratives are proceeded with long haul by means of updates and pamphlets. This is an extraordinary method for running an email crusade, for instance, HootSuite. These accounts should be well-altered to keep up with a similar voice. Posts like this additionally make extraordinary substance for virtual entertainment, This is ideal for a digital marketing campaign that is well-organized and well-maintained.

Here's the accompanying five stages that help to make stories you make to be noteworthy and interesting to clients.

Show Sympathy

Sympathy is the second thing you really want to think about often, you want to ensure that your clients comprehend that you give it a second thought. "Individuals couldn't care less about the amount you know until they know the amount that you give a second thought."

Similar to Theodore Roosevelt, you must begin demonstrating empathy to your clients. Likewise, guarantee them that you don't believe the client should feel like you're in a superior and greater circumstance in correlation than they are, yet you maintain that they should feel like, "Hello, I'm on a level battleground with you. I know precisely the exact thing you're going through. I know how you feel."

I must say that empathizing works almost everywhere, not just in business. Along these lines, why not use it to win clients

Catch Their Eye

At the point when you recount a story, you actually need to keep individuals' capacity to focus and ensure that they are at first intrigued to the point of beginning perusing the story. You can do this by utilizing Name Check to ensure your items have names that tempt the general population and utilizing Simple Word Build up to ensure your substance finds the ideal equilibrium as far as length that is interesting to your users. You additionally need to ensure that your story is impeccably written to truly spellbind your peruser and guarantee that they trust in the thing you're selling and really care about the result of the story.

Any story you tell, you want to ensure that it is successful and is creating the ideal outcomes with your clients. Notice is one approach to acquiring bits of knowledge into how your substance is driving traffic towards your site and *BuzzSumo* assists you with checking your own substance as well as your rival's substance. Without checking to ensure that you truly are building a profound association, your accounts might wallow and not have the impact you want.

You want to dissect every one of the information you can to improve and keep your perusers intrigued.

Building a close to home association by means of stories is an astonishing approach to advancing your image, and it's simplified by following the means portrayed previously.

Key Number Seven

Credibility

Any persona or character you make ought to turn into a piece of your plan of action, and you ought to expect to satisfy your commitments. This implies that you satisfy your own commitments and display how you truly esteem your clients or utilize the items you're selling. Since people now have a knack for recognizing fake advertising, you need to be sincere. Utilizing Rapportive can assist you with associating with individuals rapidly and successfully in the event that looks like the substance you're sharing.

Authenticity will be thoroughly examined in this key number seven: what it is, what it involves, and how we can be more true in our own lives.

At any point do you feel as though you're wearing a veil? Maybe you feel that you need to add a specific strategy for getting around your client or direct specific sentiments toward your partners, so that you'll be acknowledged. Rather than acting naturally, you're assuming a part to fit in, or to dazzle others. Majority of us have gone through occasions such as this. Rather than acting in a certified manner, we let individuals know what we think they need to hear, and act in manners that conflict with our real essence. So, we're living inauthentically.

Living and working this way is tiring, discouraging, and binding. It can likewise keep us away from arriving at our actual potential. Something contrary to this is to live and work legitimately. We can live without the ideas and expectations of others and choose our own path in life when we give ourselves permission to be who we are.

We will examine authenticity in depth in this article: what it is, what it involves, and how we can be more credible in our own lives.

Authenticity: What Is It?

It can appear to be that there are however many various meanings or validness as there are analysts, rationalists, and researchers. Nonetheless, a typical definition is that being real is carrying on with your life as indicated by your own qualities and objectives, instead of those of others.

Simply put, authenticity is being true to one's own personality, values, and spirit in the face of pressure to act otherwise. You're straightforward with yourself and with others, and you get a sense of ownership with your slip-ups. Your qualities, beliefs, and activities adjust. Accordingly, you seem to be certified, and you're willing to acknowledge the results of being consistent with what you view as right.

Why Be Valid?

It is generally difficult to legitimately live. On occasion, being consistent with what you know is correct implies that you conflict with the group. It might mean being unpredictable, opening yourself up for the chance of others harming you, and taking the harder street.

On one hand, it implies botching a few valuable open doors - you really do need to acknowledge this. However, in the long run, it is likely to provide numerous additional opportunities; opportunities that would simply not be available to a person who has been perceived as inconsistent, shifty, vacillating, or unauthentic.

Carrying on with a credible life is likewise immensely more compensating than concealing your actual self. You don't have to worry about what you said or didn't say, how you acted, or whether you did the right thing when you live authentically. Living legitimately implies you can trust yourself and your inspirations verifiably.

A few different advantages of being legitimate include.

Trust and regard: When you are true to who you are, not only do you trust your decisions and judgments, but also other people do the same. Because you stand by your values and beliefs, they will respect you.

Integrity: At the point when you're bonafide, you additionally have honesty. You feel free to do the correct thing, so don't need to re-think yourself. What your identity is, what you do, and what you trust in - these adjust impeccably.

Capacity to manage issues: At the point when you're straightforward with yourself as well as other people, you have the strength and receptiveness to manage issues rapidly, rather than lingering, or disregarding them by and large.

Acknowledging potential: At the point when you trust yourself and do what you know is correct, you can understand your maximum capacity throughout everyday life. You take charge of your life and stop relying on the advice of others.

Certainty and confidence: You can trust yourself to go with the ideal choices while you're being certified and making the best decision. Thus, this prompts higher fearlessness and confidence, more prominent idealism, and more life fulfillment.

Less pressure: How might you feel if, consistently, you expressed whatever you might be thinking, remained consistent with yourself, and acted likewise? Envision the joy and sense of pride you'd feel! Being real to yourself is definitely less unpleasant than being somebody else.

Be consistent with yourself; genuineness fabricates trust.

It's a significant inquiry, particularly since a considerable lot of us appear to have apparently clashing "selves." In a part named "Credibility" in the 2001 book "Handbook of Positive Brain research," Dr. Susan Harter contends that our characters can't be "fixed." Thus, we should be adaptable, and this adaptability can permit us to change and develop and acknowledge new open doors.

In any case, our actual self continues as before regardless of what circumstance we're in. Since we have various parts to play doesn't imply that we need to wear various covers to en route.

Live By Your Qualities

Living really implies that you live as per the qualities and convictions that you hold generally dear, and that the individual objectives that you seek after rise up out of these. Your initial step is to distinguish your basic beliefs, and afterward to focus on living and working as per them. You then, at that point, need to define individual objectives and profession objectives that line up with these.

Here and there you could need to settle on a morally difficult choice; This is the time when being aware of your core values will help you act ethically.

Identify the Gap Is there a gap between the person you know you could be and the person you are now? (Check for the book "Like like a Movie ")

For example, do you put on a veil when you're working? Maybe you're more rough with your group than you might want to be, on the grounds that you imagine that is the means by which a pioneer finishes things. Perhaps you embrace a sassy demeanor, since you don't believe others should imagine that you're exhausting, on the grounds that you take a serious disposition to your work. Or on the other hand, perhaps you're overflowing with thoughts that you never share, since you're worried about the possibility that your group will destroy them, and this leaves you feeling smothered and despondent.

Attempt to distinguish these holes by composing a rundown of words that depict the characteristics of the individual you realize you can be, and by contemplating how intently these reflect how you really are.

Then, at that point, pick a single word from this rundown that you need to begin dealing with - for example, maybe you need to be more "open." Utilize individual objective setting procedures, and make plans to deal with this consistently. It's more practical to lay out little objectives and work on each quality in turn than it is to attempt to change as long as you can remember, at the same time.

Developing and maintaining integrity takes courage. Begin by investigating your day to day decisions. You will frequently instinctively understand what the good and bad decisions are: you want to figure out how to pay attention to that "little voice" - that feeling of disquiet - that lets you know that something is off-base. Consider each decision you make and consider which one will make you feel better about yourself the following day.

Additionally, Honest living implies that you get a sense of ownership with your activities, including your mix-ups. Own up to your decisions, and work vigorously to right any weaknesses.

Impart Genuinely

Fair correspondence includes expressing whatever you might be thinking, while at the same time regarding the other individual's requirements and sentiments. This takes the ability to appreciate anyone at their core and great relational abilities.

Additionally, it means avoiding games: You don't use cryptic hints or other tactics to get your point across; you speak up. You can get more familiar with the mystery games that individuals can play, and how to try not to play them,

Honest communication also means keeping promises if you make a promise to someone, treat it like a bond. Never make a commitment that you can't keep because it will affect your brand or image.

Deal with Your Feelings

At this point, you consider others' requirements and as well give a valiant effort to treat them with graciousness and regard. In upsetting circumstances, this implies knowing how to get a grip on your feelings; it could also be regarded as having Emotional quotients. This is a significant piece of living truly, in light of the fact that it shows that you have internal strength and regard for everyone around you, and it's an expertise worth creating since it will work well for you in all parts of your life and profession.

Key Number Eight

Organize and Connect

Construct areas of strength for an organization both on the web and offline

One important skill that can help you advance professionally and socially is networking. In this section, we will discuss some of the dos and don'ts of professionally connecting with others and the best ways to network—both online and offline.

What is Organizing?

Extensively characterized, organizing is the most common way of building and keeping up with commonly useful expert associations with others, sometimes it's called networking..

They can be both formal and casual. Customarily it's a blend of the two, with a great deal of expert systems administration occurring in relaxed environments, both on the web and offline This can be through email, LinkedIn, in-person organizing occasions, and the sky's the limit from there.

Beginning to organize while you are at college or tertiary Institutions is the most ideal way to do this. networking is important If done well, it will give you an advantage over your competitors throughout your career. It may be the contrast between essentially following your vocation and succeeding in your picked field.

This is on the grounds that being associated with is connected to progress, permitting you to draw upon the assets, information, and abilities of your organization of experts as well as the other way around. Organizing is the instrument experts use to get associated with credible individuals of like minds

For understudies, specifically, organizing is a method for building associations with individuals that will enhance your expert life. Even while you're actually contemplating, it is great to associate with your teachers. For global understudies particularly, building an expert organization will help launch your profession after college as well as work on your relational abilities.

The following are ten hints on how you can construct serious areas of strength for an organization, both on the web and offline:

Go to industry occasions and gatherings: This is an extraordinary method for meeting and associating with different experts in your field. You can often attend workshops and networking sessions at these events to help you make new connections.

Join proficient affiliations: gain admittance to an organization of similar experts in your field. Find associations, both local and national, that align with your career objectives and interests.

Use LinkedIn: utilized appropriately, it's an incredible asset for building your expert organization. Associate with partners, industry pioneers, and others in your field. Make certain to stay up with the latest and draw in with others by sharing applicable substance and taking part in bunch conversations.

Volunteer locally: meet new people and help your community at the same time. Make it a stride further by searching for chances to chip in for occasions and causes connected with your industry. In any case, don't expect quick settlements - and just work since you will really appreciate what you're doing. Individuals will detect an essential worker - one who is just looking for their opportunity to underwrite - a pretty far.

Go to graduated class occasions: you'll meet individuals who have comparative foundations and encounters and might have the option to help you in your profession.

Go to nearby business occasions: look at your nearby office of trade or other business associations to find organizing occasions in your space. These frequently draw in different experts, from business visionaries to corporate chiefs.

Be proactive: Don't just wait for people to come up to you. Step up to the plate and acquaint yourself with others and initiate discussions. Discuss their work, interests, and objectives with them. Also, pay attention to their responses.

Follow up: in the wake of meeting another person, circle back to them by means of email or LinkedIn. Remind them of your meeting and suggest a follow-up call or meeting to continue the conversation.

Act naturally: or on the other hand as the adage goes, 'act naturally - every other person is taken'. Individuals are bound to associate with you assuming you're certifiable and genuine. Make sure to share your character and interests alongside your expert objectives.

Go to industry occasions, join pertinent gatherings, and associate with similar people

.

Organizing tips

Present yourself accurately: while cold messaging or DMing somebody, it's critical to do so expertly. Keep up with great decorum and attempt to keep things short.

Network online as though you were disconnected: online stages are presently developing to turn out to be more similar to offline connections. Conferencing programming, for instance, permits individuals to look into your home or workplace. Keeping up with a similar degree of impressive skill on the web, regardless of the areas you are viewed as an expert yourself.

Even though networking takes time and pushes you out of your comfort zone, there are numerous advantages.

Ready to elevate your brand impact's Now?

Key points;

- Go to industry occasions to gain associations, join proficient relationship for a steady networking
- influence LinkedIn to connect with friends
- volunteer locally to have a constructive outcome. By incorporating these practices,your association can flourish both on the web and offline cultivating a hearty local area and making enduring worth.

Key Number Nine

Persistent Improvement

Having mastered the crucial act of networking, leverage it and remain informed about industry patterns and improve your abilities. Monitoring changes or updates inside your industry can assist with keeping you on top of things. You will begin to equip yourself with knowledge that you can apply to your career by actively seeking out new information and remaining up to date on the latest developments.

It doesn't have to be hard to stay current in your sector. Here is some direction on how this could help your advancement and how to execute this into your work environment.

There are many advantages of staying up to date on your industry's news and trends Regardless of your position or field, staying up to date on industry news and trends will help you gain experience, identify growth opportunities, and give you an advantage over your competitors. You will continuously profit from keeping on top of your industry, whether you have recently begun in your industry or you're hoping to advance inside your job.

Distinguishing key changes, industry developments, new innovations or strategic policies can assist you with pursuing better choices quicker.

Likewise, the trust and regard your friends will have for your degree of ability will likewise assist with opening entryways for you inside your industry, molding your profession movement. Search out a tutor or industry pal

Enrolling the assistance of a tutor or a companion who works in a similar industry allows you the opportunity to learn new ideas in a group environment. This present circumstance removes you from a conventional climate and can empower a conversational stream, with the valuable chance to pose inquiries without judgment. This can assist you with developing your industry information and see things according to another point of view.

Further education or training in a course can be a great way to learn new skills that can help you advance in your career or refresh the skills you need for your job. You can continue working while taking part-time training or education courses online. Investigate what choices are out there, you could investigate courses straightforwardly connected with your industry, Share your insight through satisfied creation and conversations

You might need to ask what is Information sharing?

Information sharing is the most common way of trading data, experiences, or aptitude between people or gatherings. It includes sending what one knows to other people, either officially or casually, to improve understanding and add to aggregate information. This sharing can happen through different means, including composed or spoken correspondence, cooperative exercises, online courses and associations inside networks. The objective is to work with learning, critical thinking, and advancement by dispersing information among people or across associations. You should comprehend that Information sharing itself is unique in relation to content creation.

The process of creating and making content for a specific audience or purpose, such as text, images, videos, or multimedia, is called content creation. This content can be made for different stages, including sites, web-based entertainment, online journals, or other computerized mediums

This is the way they are separated

Content Creation:

Focus: Fundamentally revolves around delivering material in different organizations.

Purpose: aims to produce content that is entertaining, informative, or engaging for a particular audience.

Mediums: Includes the age of content, like articles, recordings, pictures, or different types of media.

Information Sharing:

Focus: emphasizes the sharing of knowledge, insights, or skills.

Purpose: aims to spread knowledge, encourage learning, and help people understand one another.

Mediums: Uses different channels, including content creation, conversations, cooperation, and different techniques to share information.

This is the way to share your insight through satisfied manifestations

Publishing content to a blog: Share insights and useful information in informative blog posts on topics that interest you.

Podcasting: Engage listeners and impart knowledge through spoken word discussions.

Video Content: Produce instructive recordings, instructional exercises, or narratives to outwardly pass on data.

Online Entertainment: Utilizing platforms like Twitter, Instagram, or LinkedIn, disseminate bite-sized knowledge and encourage discussion.

Gatherings and Online People group: Partake in conversations on discussions or online networks connected with your field, responding to questions and sharing experiences.

Online classes and Studios: Lead live meetings to educate and associate with a crowd of people progressively.

digital books and Guides: Aggregate your mastery into downloadable digital books or guides, offering exhaustive data.

Cooperative Stages: Add to cooperative stages like Wikipedia or GitHub, offering information to a more extensive crowd.

Online Courses: Create and offer seminars on stages like Coursera, Udemy, or Workable, skillshare and more

Guest Lectures: Take part as an invited speaker in online courses, digital recordings, or occasions to impart your insight to various crowds.

Note cultivating open conversations and empowering questions can upgrade the growth opportunity for both you and your crowd.

Key Number Ten

Seek for Criticism and Reviews

Look for criticism and surveys for development.

Try not to trust that input or reviews will come to you, request it consistently and from various sources. You can look for criticism from your associates, clients, tutors, or family peers. Requesting input shows that you are anxious to learn, open to valuable analysis, and ready to move along. It likewise assists you with distinguishing your assets and regions for development, and to adjust your assumptions to other people.

Moreso, Input is certainly not a one-time occasion, however a consistent interaction. You ought to audit criticism intermittently to screen your improvement, to praise your triumphs, and to recognize new regions for advancement. You ought to likewise look for input again to quantify your advancement, to approve your activities, and to change your arrangement if necessary. Evaluating input intermittently assists you with supporting your improvement, to keep up with your inspiration, and to accomplish your objectives.

You should comprehend that When you get criticism, you need to listen cautiously and consciously. Try not to intrude, contend, or get protective. Attempt to comprehend the viewpoint and goal of the individual giving you input, and pose explaining inquiries if necessary. Paying attention to input mindfully assists you with valuing the worth of the criticism, to recognize your accomplishments and difficulties, and to keep away from miscommunication or misconception

Continuously recollect that Criticism is pointless on the off chance that you don't follow up on it expeditiously. Create a strategy for putting the feedback's suggestions into action after you've considered it. Set explicit, quantifiable, attainable, important, and time-bound (Shrewd) objectives and keep tabs on your development. You can improve your results, demonstrate your appreciation for the feedback, and demonstrate your commitment to improvement by responding to feedback promptly.

Feedback is a two-way street, and you can also help other people improve their skills and performance by giving them feedback. Notwithstanding, giving input usefully requires a few abilities and civility. You ought to give input that is ideal, explicit, legit, deferential, and steady. You ought to likewise adjust positive and pessimistic input, center around the way of behaving and not the individual, and use models and proof.

Appreciate and Value Your Crowd

Always show appreciation for your audience and engage with them. Here are the steps to do that *personalization*: Tailor your collaborations to the interests and inclinations of your crowd. Customized reactions cause people to feel seen and heard.

Offer Thanks: Thank your audience for their support on a regular basis. Whether it's through devoted appreciation posts or essentially saying thanks to them in your substance, it supports a positive association.

Have round table Discussions: Once in a while Coordinate back and forth discussions, either live or through different stages, to straightforwardly address your crowd's requests and make a more intelligent encounter.

Use Online Entertainment, recognize Commitments, however, Responding promptly to messages and comments on social media platforms is a great way to connect with your audience. One more method for showing appreciation for your crowd's unwaveringly is to answer immediately to their remarks and messages via web-based entertainment. This demonstrates that you value their interaction and care about their opinions, feedback, questions, and concerns. Participating in discussions, retweeting or sharing relevant content, and responding to comments and messages can also help you resolve any issues or complaints that may arise. You can utilize virtual entertainment instruments, for example, ***chatbots***, ***autoresponders***, or layouts to mechanize a portion of your reactions, yet make a point to add a personalization and human touch to cause them to feel true and certifiable.

Local area Building: Cultivate a feeling of local area among your crowd. Urge them to associate with one another, share their encounters, and construct connections inside the local area.

Reward them with selective offers: Rewarding your audience's loyalty with exclusive offers, discounts, freebies, or other perks is another way to show your appreciation. Just like I added a little bit of reward in this book just to appreciate you for trusting me to Guide you. This can assist you in attracting new followers who wish to join your VIP club as well as in increasing your retention, loyalty, and advocacy rates. You can utilize online entertainment to compensate your steadfast devotees by making unwaveringly programs, reference projects, giveaways, or challenges that reward them for their commitment, buys, or references. You can likewise utilize online entertainment to report, advance, or convey your prizes, and to thank your dependable adherents for their help.

Share in the background content: Sharing behind-the-scenes content that gives them a glimpse into your brand's personality, culture, values, as you can see I started by telling a bit of my background in the beginning of this book and procedures is another way to show your appreciation for your audience's loyalty. This can assist you with acculturating your image, fortify your relationship with your crowd, and increment your straightforwardness and believability. You can utilize virtual entertainment to share in the background content by posting stories, live recordings, reels, or webcasts that exhibit your group, your workplace, your activities, your difficulties, or your accomplishments. You can likewise utilize virtual entertainment to request your crowd's feedback, criticism, or ideas on your in the background content, and to include them in your dynamic cycle

Praise achievements and accomplishments: More ways of showing appreciation for your crowd's steadfastness is to perceive and commend your achievements and accomplishments with them. This can assist you with recognizing their commitment to your prosperity, offer your thanks and appreciation, and offer your energy and bliss. You can utilize online entertainment to praise your achievements and accomplishments by posting declarations, recordings, pictures, or infographics that feature your key measurements, objectives, or results. You can likewise utilize virtual entertainment to welcome your crowd to join your festival, to share their own accounts or tributes, or to offer them an extraordinary arrangement or compensation for being important for your excursion. Whether it's arriving at a devotee count, commemoration, or individual accomplishments, share the delight with your local area.

Expand Content Sorts: Offer various substance types to take care of various inclinations. This could incorporate composed articles, recordings, infographics, or even intuitive tests to keep things fascinating.

Influence Client Reviews: Producing relevant and useful content that informs, entertains, educates, or inspires your audience is one way to show your appreciation for their loyalty. This shows that you grasp their requirements, interests, difficulties, and goals, and that you need to furnish them with helpful and significant data. You can also improve your social media performance by creating content that is valuable and pertinent, which can increase your reach, engagement, traffic, and conversions. You can utilize web-based entertainment to make significant and applicable substance by utilizing client overviews to lead research , reviews, surveys, or meetings to figure out what your crowd needs to learn, see, or hear from you, and by utilizing various configurations, styles, and tones to suit their inclinations and assumptions. Utilize the bits of knowledge to tailor your substance and commitment techniques.

Organize Live Events: Put together live streams, online classes, or virtual occasions where you can straightforwardly communicate with your crowd. This constant commitment makes a dynamic and vivid experience.

Energize Client Created Difficulties: Client produced content (UGC) is any content made by your crowd that elements or notices your image, for example, photographs, recordings, surveys, or tributes. UGC is a strong way to feature your crowd's steadfastness and fulfillment, as well as to move others to join your local area. You can utilize web-based entertainment to feature UGC by reposting, sharing, or remarking on it, and by giving credit and applause to the first makers. By creating hashtags, challenges, contests, or campaigns that encourage your audience to participate and share their experiences with your brand, you can also encourage more UGC.

Make a Devotion Program: Carry out a steadfastness program or advantages for your most drawn in crowd individuals. This could incorporate selective substance, early access, or extraordinary limits.

Adjust to Criticism: Follow up on valuable criticism from your crowd. Exhibiting that you tune in and adjust in light of their feedback, it fortifies the association and shows that their perspectives matter.

<u>Conclusion</u>

As we reach the final pages of "Keys on How to Become a Brand," I want to acknowledge the incredible journey you've undertaken. This isn't just a book; it's a compass guiding you through the labyrinth of self-discovery and brand transformation.

Discovering Your Essence: In the quiet moments of self-reflection, you've uncovered the magic within you. Your strengths, skills, and values are not just words on paper; they are the foundation of the remarkable brand you're building. Embrace this uniqueness; it's the spark that sets your brand ablaze.

Crafting a Melody of Stories: Your brand story is a melody, and each chapter resonates with authenticity and purpose. The journey from defining your brand to communicating transformation is not just about words; it's about creating a melody that echoes in the hearts of those who connect with your brand.

Capturing Hearts and Minds: *Understanding your audience is like an art dance* where you connect, resonate, and empathize. By providing solutions and articulating their challenges, you've not just captured attention; you've captured hearts. Your brand is now a part of their stories.

Digital Footprints and Beyond: Your online presence is not a mere digital footprint; it's a testament to your brand's soul. You've mastered the art of being seen, heard, and understood. Your digital spaces are not just platforms; they are stages where your brand performs its unique dance.

The Eternal Growth Spiral: As you close this chapter, remember that the journey of a brand is an eternal spiral of growth. Continuous improvement is the mantra. Stay hungry for knowledge, share your wisdom, and let your brand evolve. Seek feedback, for it is the compass that guides you toward excellence.

Gratitude and Connection: Express gratitude for your audience and the community that has embraced your brand. Every review, every comment, is a testament to the connections you've forged. Your brand is not just a name; it's a shared experience, a community.

Your Brand Legacy: "Keys on How to Become a Brand" is not just a book; it's a guide to crafting a legacy. Your brand is now a living entity, ready to script new chapters. So, with the keys firmly in your grasp, step forward into the unknown – for your brand, your odyssey, has just begun.

May your brand continue to shine, evolve, and inspire.

Warmest Regards,

Diane A. Gandara

<u>NOTES</u>

About the Author

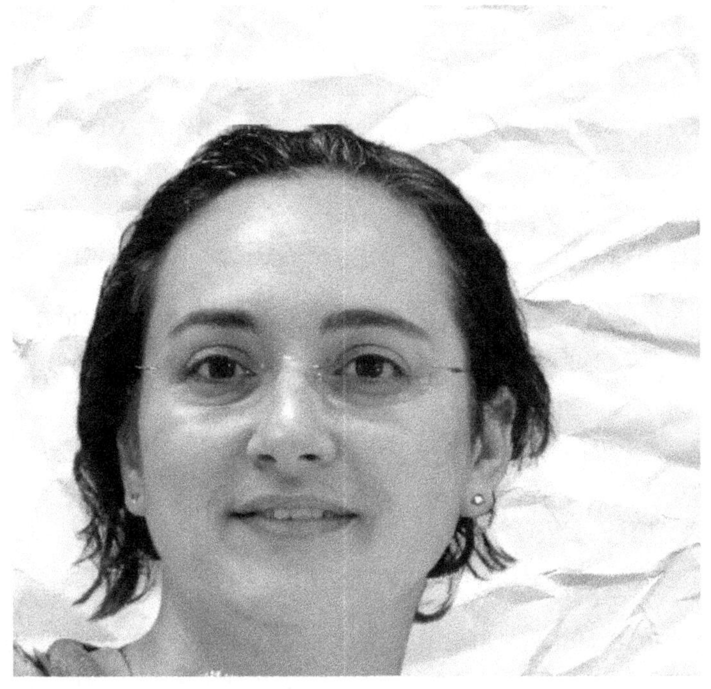

Diane A. Gandara's journey as an author and digital entrepreneur is marked by a commitment to bridging the gap between technology and personal development. As a computer scientist, she navigates the digital landscape with precision, offering practical advice on leveraging online platforms for professional growth.

Diane's expertise extends to the art of branding, where she becomes a guiding force for individuals seeking to establish and refine their personal brand. Her insights into the dynamics of effective branding are not only informed by her technical background but also enriched by a keen understanding of human behavior and communication.

In the realm of personal and professional development, Diane's work becomes a roadmap for those navigating the complexities of career advancement and self-discovery. Her writing delves into topics such as Life like a movie , Growth, leadership

resilience, and adaptability, providing readers with actionable strategies to thrive in a rapidly evolving digital landscape.

A true advocate for empowerment, Diane A. Gandara stands out not only as an accomplished computer scientist and digital entrepreneur but also as a thought leader who shares insights and encourages others to embrace the intersection of technology and personal growth. Through her books, she sparks inspiration and guides individuals on a transformative journey toward unlocking their full potential.

Diane empowers individuals by enhancing their online presence. Through her writings, , and successful branding, creating a unique blend that resonates with a diverse audience.

<u>Review Page</u>

Dear recipient,

I trust you're doing well! I'd like to express my immense gratitude for delving into "Keys on How to Become a Personal Brand." Your time and commitment mean a great deal to me!

If you've discovered any valuable insights, felt inspired, or perhaps even had a good time, could you please share your impressions with a brief review? Your perspective on the book could significantly impact others contemplating taking the plunge.

Whether you choose to unveil your thoughts on platforms like Amazon, extend a shoutout on Goodreads, or share your reflections wherever you connect online, linkedin, YouTube,

Facebook, or even mai…your words possess extraordinary influence!

A heartfelt thank you once more for being part of this journey. Your review serves as the special ingredient that enhances the entire personal branding adventure!

Best regards,

Diane A. Gandara

Author of the book "Keys on How to Become a Brand."

Recommended Resources and Tools

Online Courses:

Coursera: "Brand Management: Aligning Business, Brand, and Behaviour" (sponsored by the University of London)

Websites and Blogs:

  - Awwwards (awwwards.com): For inspiration on web design and creative branding.

Facebook page

 Talks about branding and self development by Princess Blessing

YouTube channel

De-Best Digital Consults; Focuses on Creating your online presence and personalized resource's

Tools:

  Canva (canva.com): A user-friendly design tool for creating logos, social media graphics, and other branding materials.

Brandfolder (brandfolder.com): A platform for managing and sharing brand assets.

Communities:

- Branding subreddit (reddit.com/r/branding): Engage with discussions and seek advice from the branding community on Reddit.

***Automation Tools
for Appointment***

Calendly.com

Google forms

Luna.com etc

For Email automation

Mail chimp

Active Campaign

Flodesk

For Lead Generation

Brizzy Pro

Elementor

System.io

For Chat box automation for client Support and Engagement

Drift

Many chat

Joinchat for WhatsApp

Hot Live

Chat Baby

Chat Node

For Social Media

Content Studio

Buffer etc

For Proposal or Invoice

Waves Apps etc

For E-commerce

Shopify

Selar.co

WordPress

Woo Commerce

Hook commerce

Aleph Express

Ebay

Amazon etc

For payments

Paypal

Stripe

Flutter wave

Paystack Etc

Remember to tailor your resources based on your specific branding needs and objectives.